Contents

Some words are printed in bold, **like this**. You can find out what they mean by looking in the glossary.

What is processed food?

Today, there are more people to feed around the world than ever before. In **developed countries**, even people living in small towns have access to thousands of different food products.

Most people like having a choice about the foods they eat, and processing foods into different products provides that. Processing has also made many foods more affordable for a wider range of people. Poor people often can more readily buy a tin of vegetables than the same amount of fresh produce from a local farm. But critics say processed foods can present health problems, because they are loaded with ingredients known to cause disease. Fat, salt, and sugar are at the top of the "danger" list. Processed foods can be both a benefit and a risk.

Almost everything we eat requires some sort of processing. For example, you cannot eat a grain of wheat. Rather, the wheat needs to be **milled** into flour, and the flour then needs to be combined with other ingredients and baked in an oven before it becomes bread.

What is processing?

Processing occurs in many ways for different reasons. Canning or freezing fruits or vegetables helps preserve them. They last longer on a shop's shelf than they could if they were left as they were when they were harvested. Drying certain foods, such as meats and fruit, serves the same purpose. Meals packaged in tins or cartons give shoppers an easy way to eat a variety of foods without having to take the time to follow recipes. Some of these packaged foods can also be eaten far from the kitchen, making them useful for people who are on the go. Some processing can make foods safer to eat. Milk, for example, is **pasteurized**, a process that kills harmful organisms. Processed foods are common, and often cheap and convenient. Recently, however, some food experts have said that people eat too many processed foods.

Processing is not always a bad thing. Some fruits and vegetables are better tasting and even healthier if processed in some way. For example, freezing is often a good form of processing. If vegetables are frozen in the correct way, they retain their vitamins. This makes them healthier to eat than unprocessed vegetables that have been sitting in a shop for several days. But, as we will see, many other foods are processed to the point of not only losing all their nutritional value, but also of becoming unsafe to eat.

Ethics of Food

Processing Your Food

John Bliss

www.raintreepublishers.co.uk
Visit our website to find out more information about Raintree books.

To order:
☎ Phone 0845 6044371
📄 Fax +44 (0) 1865 312263
✉ Email myorders@raintreepublishers.co.uk

Customers from outside the UK please telephone +44 1865 312262

Raintree is an imprint of Capstone Global Library Limited, a company incorporated in England and Wales having its registered office at 7 Pilgrim Street, London, EC4V 6LB – Registered company number: 6695582

Text © Capstone Global Library Limited 2012
First published in hardback in 2012
Paperback edition first published in 2013
The moral rights of the proprietor have been asserted.

Edited by Adam Miller, Andrew Farrow, and Adrian Vigliano
Designed by Ryan Frieson
Illustrated by Mapping Specialists Ltd and Planman Technologies
Picture research by Tracy Cummins
Originated by Capstone Global Library Ltd
Printed and bound in China by Leo Paper Products Ltd

ISBN 978 1 406 22465 8 (hardback)
15 14 13 12 11
10 9 8 7 6 5 4 3 2 1

ISBN 978 1 406 22471 9 (paperback)
16 15 14 13 12
10 9 8 7 6 5 4 3 2 1

British Library Cataloguing in Publication Data
Bliss, John
Processing your food. – (Ethics of food)
174.9'664-dc22
A full catalogue record for this book is available from the British Library.

Acknowledgements
We would like to thank the following for permission to reproduce photographs: AP Photo p. 13 (Mark Humphrey); Corbis pp. 11 (© Corbis), 21 (© Dominique Derda), 35 (© Bettmann), 42 (© TWPhoto); Food Standards Agency p. 50 bottom (food.gov.uk); Getty Images pp. 6 (DEA/G. Lovera), 9 (Miguel Villagran), 20 (Graeme Robertson), 25 (Brandi Simons), 26 (Hans Neleman); istockphoto p. 18 (© Aleaimage); Library of Congress Prints and Photographs Division p. 38; mypyramid.gov p. 50 top; Rex Features p. 28 (C. Magnolia/Everett); Shutterstock pp. 5 (© Morgan Lane Photography), 17 (© Dmitriy Kuzmichev), 23 (© Picsfive), 27 (© Helga Esteb), 30 (© Alen), 32 (© 29september), 36 (© Picsfive), 41 (© Kheng Guan Toh), 44 (© Dmitry Kalinovsky), 46 (© Noam Wind).

Cover photograph of a pig being processed reproduced with permission of Getty Images (Scott Olson).

We would like to thank Christopher Nicolson for his invaluable help in the preparation of this book.

Every effort has been made to contact copyright holders of any material reproduced in this book. Any omissions will be rectified in subsequent printings if notice is given to the publisher.

Disclaimer
All the Internet addresses (URLs) given in this book were valid at the time of going to press. However, due to the dynamic nature of the Internet, some addresses may have changed, or sites may have changed or ceased to exist since publication. While the author and publisher regret any inconvenience this may cause readers, no responsibility for any such changes can be accepted by either the author or the publisher.

Fresh vegetables are a great food choice, if they're available. In some places, vegetables that have been processed and tinned are the only option for shoppers.

The history of processed food

People have been cooking food for over two million years. Cooking is a basic kind of food processing. Beyond that, the first kinds of food processing were probably used to make beer and bread. Both were invented about 10,000 years ago. Here, simple grains were processed into new foods or drinks that no longer resembled the original source. The role of yeast, which turns grain into beer, was probably an accidental discovery.

Over time, many methods of food processing were developed to preserve foods. Before refrigeration, people had to find ways to store foods that could spoil, such as meats, fruits, and vegetables. Meats were preserved through salting and air **curing** at least 2,500 years ago. (With air curing, the air itself dries the food to preserve it. Other forms of curing use chemicals to do the same thing.)

The Romans enjoyed sausages and other cured meats. Salted fish, such as cod, were a mainstay of travellers in the 16th century, and native peoples in both South and North America made versions of dried meat. Even fruitcake was invented as a way of preserving fruits and nuts. In the early 19th century, canning was invented as a way to process food so that it could be preserved.

Ancient Egyptians were familiar with the process of using grain and fruit to make beer and wine.

Modern processing techniques

Today, some of these traditional methods of preservation are still used. But many have been replaced by using chemicals and other food **additives**. One of the oldest **preservatives**, salt, is still used today. It's sometimes listed on food labels as some form of **sodium**. The human body needs some salt to function properly. But the large amounts found in some processed foods can increase the risk of high blood pressure, which can lead to heart-related diseases.

Other common preservatives are nitrates and nitrites. Nitrates appear naturally in many vegetables. When added to food, especially meats, they help keep them from spoiling. But some experts say too many nitrates and nitrites could raise the risk of cancer. Others say these are safe at the levels used in food processing.

Two related chemicals called BHT and BHA are found in many foods. They help stop the fats found in foods from going bad. Processed foods are often high in fat, because food companies know humans are drawn to it. It adds flavour to food. Like salt, some fat is necessary for a healthy body. But the level of fat in processed foods is too high, a British government health institute said in 2010. The BHA and BHT added to foods may also pose health risks. Large doses have led to cancer in rats.

Other substances added to food include different fats. But one kind, called **trans fats**, is particularly unhealthy. Trans fats are found in oils called **partially hydrogenated oils**. These oils help preserve the food so it can sit longer on a shelf, and they appear in such products as margarine, baked goods, and snack foods. But trans fats have been linked to heart disease.

Many processed foods also lack something helpful to humans – **fibre**. Fruits, vegetables, and grains contain fibre, which helps the body to digest food and may reduce the risk of certain cancers. Processing these foods removes or reduces the fibre in them.

Some additives are natural and pose no health risks. Citric acid, for example, comes from citrus fruits. It's added to certain foods to keep their level of acid stable. Folic acid, a type of B vitamin, is added to certain foods because it has health benefits. The vitamin helps prevent heart disease. But some doctors and food experts worry about the additives and preservatives that may damage a person's health. They argue that people should eat fewer processed foods so they can avoid these harmful ingredients. Eating more fresh food from local sources is one way to do this. But food companies and others argue that not all people have access to that kind of food – or can afford it.

Processing grains

Flour is a staple of human existence. All western cultures enjoy some kind of bread, and for many years, bread was at the centre of people's diets. But the flour used by Europeans 1,000 years ago is very different from the flour at your local supermarket today.

The basic process of milling wheat into flour is fairly simple. The grains are ground between heavy rollers, which separate the **bran**, or outer coating, from the inner wheat **kernel** and **germ**. The germ is the centre portion of the kernel, which contains the "embryo" of a new wheat plant. It also contains many important nutrients, including **protein**, vitamins, and healthy **fatty acids**. (Found in the fat of many animals and plants, fatty acids have many health benefits. Omega-3, for example, helps the brain function well.) In the past, when wheat was ground between stone wheels, the germ was crushed and became part of the rest of the milled kernel.

But today, many people buy and eat something called white flour. In white flour, the germ has been removed. But why remove the germ? The germ contains oils, which can go bad. By removing the germ, the shelf life of the flour is increased, meaning it can last much longer on a supermarket shelf. The process of creating white flour also removes any illness-causing mould and fungus that might be on the grains. But unfortunately, removing the germ also removes much of the nutrition.

Health watch
Bye-bye bread

In 1972, Dr Robert Atkins introduced a new diet designed to help people lose weight quickly. He stressed eating more meat and cutting down on bread, pasta, and even some vegetables. The Atkins Diet exploded in popularity during the 1990s, and many people on the diet completely stopped eating bread. Most dieters did lose weight, but many later put the pounds back on. Several doctors questioned the Atkins Diet's long-term health effects. Dr Robert H. Eckel of the University of Colorado said he and others "worry that the diet promotes heart disease ...There is also potential loss of bone, and the potential for people with liver and kidney problems to have trouble with the high amounts of protein in these diets." The Atkins Diet, however, still has many followers.

These pipes are part of a flour mill in Munich, Germany.

Flour

In the 1920s, scientists began to realize that, while processed flour did not make people ill, it was not particularly nutritious. In 1929, scientists revealed that wholemeal bread was a lot better for people's health than white bread, but people did not change their buying habits. By 1942, in the middle of World War II, white bread was no longer made because of a lack of storage for white flour. The National Loaf appeared, which was similar to today's brown bread. In 1956, new laws stated that all flour other than wholemeal had to be **fortified** with calcium, iron, and other minerals.

Golden rice

For much of the world, especially Asia, rice is the primary grain that people eat. Like white flour, white rice is created by removing the nutrient-rich husk, bran, and germ from brown rice. This is done to prevent spoiling. Unfortunately, it also removes many of the health benefits of brown rice.

Fortified food

If you look at a typical box of breakfast cereal, you will probably notice a claim such as "fortified with vitamins and minerals". When food is fortified, processing adds nutrients that were never originally in the food. Many of the foods people buy in the supermarket have been fortified. Milk is usually fortified with vitamin D, orange juice is often fortified with calcium and vitamin D, and many cereals and grain products have been fortified with other vitamins and minerals.

Why has this food been fortified? For most of history, people did not have year-round access to necessary vitamins. This was largely because fruits and vegetables do not naturally grow in all areas at all times. People often suffered from diseases like rickets, caused by a lack of vitamin D, or scurvy, caused by a lack of vitamin C.

Fortifying foods allows people to have access to necessary nutrients, even in areas where little food is grown. However, doctors and scientists are starting to wonder how useful fortification is. There is some evidence that the body does not absorb nutrients from fortified foods the same way that it does when those minerals are found in foods naturally. Some fortified foods also have so much sugar and artificial flavouring added that they cease being healthy overall.

Since the late 1990s, scientists have been working on a new form of **genetically modified (GM)** rice known as "golden rice". Golden rice contains beta-carotene, a mineral that converts to vitamin A inside the body. Scientists are creating golden rice to try to help countries where a lack of vitamin A is a problem.

However, many people object to the development of golden rice, and to plans to grow it in **developing countries**.

Some people argue that it would be better to simply help citizens of developing countries gain access to naturally occurring vitamin-rich foods in their area. They also worry that introducing a GM crop like golden rice presents the same range of issues that are connected to other GM crops. These concerns include possible health problems caused by eating these crops. (For more on GM crops, see pages 20 and 21.)

Vitamins and minerals are often added to children's cereals, but so are unnecessary colours, sugars, and flavours.

Environment watch

Is ethanol the fuel of the future?

The first Model T car designed by Henry Ford, in 1908, ran on ethanol, otherwise known as grain alcohol. Ethanol can be made from corn, wheat, grass, sugarcane, and even sawdust.

Today, ethanol is often proposed as an alternative fuel source to petroleum-based fuels like petrol. While ethanol can be made in small batches fairly easily, a lot of energy is used to produce enough ethanol to serve as a substitute for petrol. Critics argue that it actually takes more energy to produce the ethanol than it does to just use petrol.

King corn

Corn has always been an important and delicious part of many people's diets in the West. Corn was first grown in the Americas, and it later spread to Europe and northern Africa. By 1600, it had made its way to China and beyond.

Corn has always been useful. It can be eaten as a vegetable without any processing (although cooking helps), but it can also be stored and turned into a grain. It can go through a process known as **fermentation** and be turned into alcohol, including ethanol. Corn husks can be turned into fuel, or they can be used for rugs and twine. The plant's leaves also make good animal feed.

Today, believe it or not, corn is in a huge number of the products you will find in a modern supermarket – and in many products in other shops as well. Corn has become the most important grain today. But why?

Creating a new plant

You are probably familiar with the idea of dog breeds like Labradors and poodles. These are breeds that were created by mating dogs to create the most desirable traits in future dogs. More recently, existing breeds have been crossbred to create new, "hybrid" breeds like Labradoodles (Labrador plus poodle).

The same thing happens with plants. Plants can be bred in ways that create new kinds of plants or better or more useful varieties of the same plant. In some instances, creating new plants is not very profitable for large agriculture companies or seed companies. After all, once they sell people the new plant, people can use the seeds from that plant to grow their own in the future.

Small batches of ethanol can even be created fairly easily at home. But most ethanol is produced in big factories.

But, with corn, big agriculture companies discovered something important. New breeds of corn can be created in such a way that the new plants' seeds do not grow the same size of corn. So, a big company can crossbreed two varieties of corn to create a very desirable form of corn. Let's say they sell that corn to smaller farmers, who like the corn because it has big kernels. But that corn does not reproduce in the same way as other plants. This means the farmer has to buy more of the same corn from the big business every year.

Clearly, large agriculture companies can make a lot of money by creating new forms of corn. This makes them want to find new kinds of corn. Once they create the corn, they need to create more products to use those new types of corn.

Animal feed

Because it is so cheap and plentiful, people find new uses for corn. For example, it is processed into many animal feeds. Cattle, pigs, chicken, and even fish are all fed corn – even though cows and fish do not naturally eat corn (see pages 24 and 25). Those animals then become food for people, increasing the amount of corn we eat in our processed foods.

High fructose corn syrup

While it is not a major issue in the UK, the use of corn that has recently been in the news in the United States is **high fructose corn syrup (HFCS)**. It was first developed in 1957, but HFCS was not really used before the 1970s. Today, 18,000 litres of corn are turned into 8.2 billion kilograms of HFCS every year.

From the point of view of food producers, HFCS is a wonderful sugar substitute. It is inexpensive, easy to produce, and aids in keeping food moist. But there are serious downsides.

HFCS and obesity

There is a lot of conflicting information about the link between HFCS and **obesity**, or being severely overweight. It is clear that obesity rates have increased since HFCS became popular, but definitions of "obese" have also changed during this time period.

Health watch

Making HFCS

How is HFCS made? Food producers use the following steps:

1. Corn kernels are soaked in warm water containing the chemical sulphur dioxide. This makes the kernels softer and easier to separate.

2. The germ of the corn, which contains oil and nutrients, is removed (much like it is in white flour).

3. The remaining cornstarch is washed.

4. Substances called enzymes are added to break the starch into substances called glucose and **fructose**.

5. The resulting syrup goes through an evaporation process so that it becomes ideal for shipping.

Much of the information we have about HFCS comes from companies with an interest in selling either HFCS or competing products, so it can be very difficult to know what is and isn't true.

However, there are some things we do know:

- HFCS is cheaper than sugar, so products with HFCS tend to come in larger serving sizes.

- Fructose does not stimulate leptin, a **hormone** that lets people know when they are full. So, people may overeat foods with HFCS.

- HFCS is found in many products where people may not expect it to be. This means that some people who believe they are eating healthily actually are not.

Products that often contain forms of corn		
Food	Personal care	Industrial
Chewing gum	Medicines	Engine fuel
Sweets	Deodorant	Plastics
Icing	Make-up	Chemicals
Instant tea	Vitamins	Explosives
Non-dairy creamer		Shoe polish
Peanut butter		Glue
Alcohol		Fibreglass

Corn is found in food products as well as in many unexpected places. This chart shows a few of the many items that contain corn.

Health watch

Battling over HFCS

No one disputes that using HFCS makes certain foods cheaper. But its use in so many foods – and its possible role in increasing certain diseases – has raised concerns. In the United States, some people have called for banning the sale of products that contain the sugar. Rather than risk losing sales, some companies are beginning to take HFCS out of their foods and use other sugars instead. To some scientists, the larger issue is that too many people eat too much sugar in all forms.

Processing fruits and vegetables

Few things are healthier than fresh fruits and vegetables. But what happens when fruits and vegetables are processed?

From vine to tin

Let's begin by looking at the example of tomatoes. Processed tomatoes – including tinned tomatoes, ketchup, tomato paste, and tomato sauce – are a huge US business. In 2001, £141 million worth of processed tomatoes were exported to other countries. In 2007, the total value of US processed tomatoes was £557 million. California, USA, is the biggest producer of processed tomatoes.

Processed tomatoes usually have a thicker skin than fresh-market tomatoes (those that are meant to be bought raw in the shops). This is to help the tomatoes survive the mechanical harvesting and bulk transportation they undergo.

Health watch

Are tinned fruits and vegetables safe?

Many people wonder whether or not tinned fruits and vegetables are safe. In the case of tomatoes, the good news is that processed tomatoes appear to retain much of their health benefits. **Organic** products (those that are grown naturally, without chemicals) have the most lycopene and vitamins, but even non-organic tomato products have health benefits.

The bad news is that a chemical known as Bisphenol A (BPA) has been found in the linings of some tinned foods. Among the concerns about BPA is that it can cause birth defects, obesity, and **neurological** issues. Many people worry that the acid in tomatoes may cause that chemical to leak into tinned tomatoes.

In 2010 Canada became the first country to declare BPA a toxic substance. The US food company General Mills announced in 2010 that it had found an alternative lining free of BPA. Companies around the world have already begun to remove or reduce the amount of BPA in food-related products.

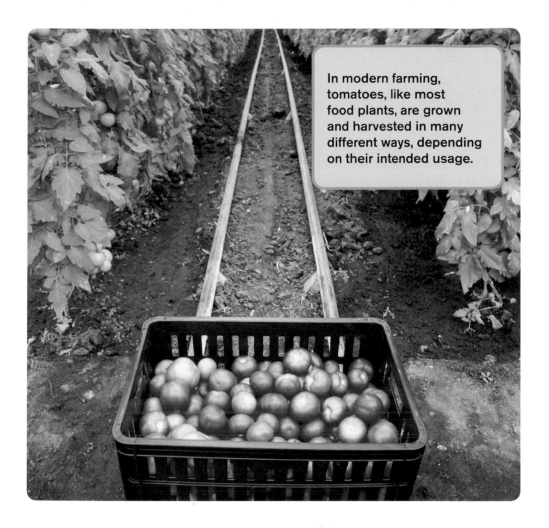

In modern farming, tomatoes, like most food plants, are grown and harvested in many different ways, depending on their intended usage.

After transportation there is a very small period of time (about six hours) to turn the fresh tomatoes into paste without spoilage or damage. This small window of time means that the manufacturing plant (factory) is usually close to where the tomatoes are grown. Once the tomatoes have been turned into paste, it can be stored for up to 18 months. The manufacturer then sells the tomato paste to other companies that add spices, flavours, and colours to turn the industrial tomato paste into products like ketchup or tomato sauce.

The demand for processed tomatoes is expected to continue to grow. This is partly because condiments like salsa and ketchup are becoming more and more popular. It is also because tomatoes are rich in vitamins A and C, as well as the **antioxidant** lycopene, which some research suggests helps prevent cancer.

Ethylene

Ethylene is the naturally occurring gas that causes fruits (like tomatoes and bananas) and vegetables to ripen and decay. But food companies have found a way to process fruits and vegetables using ethylene.

Fruits and vegetables that will be transported and sold are often picked before they are ripe. These fruits and vegetables are then exposed to human-made ethylene to aid in their ripening process. So, even some fresh fruits now undergo a form of processing before getting to your plate.

How are baby carrots "born"?

Ethylene is not the only way that fruits and vegetables have become processed. For example, "baby carrots" are not actually baby carrots. They are ordinary carrots that have been peeled, cut into short lengths, and run through a grinder. They were first introduced in the 1980s by a California farmer who was tired of discarding imperfect carrots that could not be sold in supermarkets.

Baby carrots are generally as healthy as regular carrots. Some nutrients are lost in the peeling of the carrot, but given that most people peel carrots before eating them anyway, this does not have an enormous impact on the health benefits. However, baby carrots are much more expensive than regular carrots.

Baby carrots are delicious and nutritious, but they also undergo unnecessary processing.

Health watch

Added colours

Fruit juices and tinned fruits and vegetables often have colour added. In July 2010, the European Union began requiring that the following warning be placed on six food colour additives: "Warning: Alurra Red AC E129 [or one of the other five colours] may have an adverse effect on activity and attention in children." Alurra Red is also called Red 40. The other colour addditives listed by the European Union are Ponceau 4R, Tartrazine (Yellow 5), Sunset Yellow FCF/Orange Yellow S (Yellow 6), Quinoline Yellow, and Carmoisine.

The warning labels are the result of a 2007 research study at the University of Southampton. There were two parts to the study. In one, 153 three-year-olds and 144 eight- and nine-year-olds were given one of two drink mixes containing either **synthetic** (artificial) food colours and additives or a placebo, meaning a version with nothing added. The children were drawn from the general population and across a range of hyperactivity and attention deficit/hyperactivity disorder (ADHD) levels.

Researchers eventually concluded that the artificial food colours and additives increased hyperactive behaviour in the children, at least up to middle childhood.

A more natural source

To avoid ethylene and other preservatives, some consumers choose to buy fresh, locally grown fruits and vegetables. Farmers' markets have become a popular source for those foods, as well as meat, dairy products, and other goods. Farmers within a community come to a public area, often a park, to sell their most recently harvested goods. The markets give shoppers the chance to support local people, rather than large companies that might be based thousands of kilometres away. At both these markets and in shops, some people look for organic foods. These foods are grown without any chemicals to kill insects or weeds or improve the soil. Organic meat and other animal products come from livestock fed food that does not contain chemicals. Organic foods and other food from local farms tend to be more expensive, as more work has to be done by hand. But people who can afford local or organic foods like knowing where their food comes from, and also that it does not have chemicals or preservatives in it.

GMs and Frankenfruits

Every living thing, including plants and animals, is made up of genes. These genes are passed from generation to generation and act as a code for different traits. Some of these traits are physical things, like eye colour or hair colour.

Fruits and vegetables are also made up of genes, and scientists have found ways to alter these genes to create more desirable features. For example, a farmer might want plants that are resistant to herbicides (poisons that kill plants), or that last through cold weather, or that resist insect infestation.

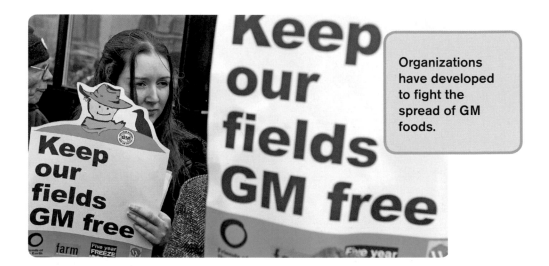

Organizations have developed to fight the spread of GM foods.

People have always altered plants through breeding. But today, scientists can actually add new genes to change a plant's genetic make-up. This process of creating new fruits and vegetables by mixing in genes from other fruits and vegetables is called genetic modification (GM). It has led to the name "Frankenfruit," which refers to the monster created by Dr Frankenstein in Mary Shelley's novel *Frankenstein*.

The first GM crops to be grown were tomatoes. These tomatoes had been modified so that they would not easily become soft. Soya beans, cotton, and corn have all also been modified for different reasons, such as heartier growth and more nutrition.

While GM foods may seem like a solution, many environmentalists and nutritionists are concerned about their side effects. For example, poisons are bred into some plants to help them resist pests. These poisons may actually be poisoning insects and butterflies.

Health watch

Helpful human-made foods

Malnutrition, meaning the lack of enough nutrients, is a huge problem in poor African nations. The problem is especially bad among young children, since malnourished mothers cannot produce enough breast milk to feed their children. Powdered milk and formula are not good substitutes, as these require water and many villages do not have clean water supplies.

A French-designed processed food called Plumpy'nut was specifically designed to help feed malnourished children in Africa. It is a combination of peanut butter, powdered milk, and powdered sugar, **enriched** with vitamins and minerals. It is sweet, so children want to eat it. It does not need to be refrigerated or cooked, so it is easy to store and serve. With this food, some malnourished children have been able to achieve a normal weight in only four weeks.

Plumpy'nut has become a life-saving product for malnourished children all over the world.

Although people do not want insects eating crops, they are still an important part of the natural order. Recent tests have shown that the crops not only poison pests that attempt to eat them, but they also leak the toxins from their roots into the ground.

Nutritionists are concerned about GM foods for two reasons. Firstly, although modifying crops may allow new nutrients to be added to foods, it may also introduce harmful chemicals.

The second concern is related to allergies. In 1992 a US company added genes from Brazil nuts to soya beans, in an attempt to create more nutritious soya beans. However, people who were allergic to Brazil nuts discovered that they were also allergic to the modified soya beans. Unless an ingredient panel lists not only every ingredient, but also how each ingredient has been modified, it could be impossible for a person with allergies to ever know if the food they are eating is safe for them.

Processing meat

Meat has long been an important part of many people's diets. Early humans were hunters and gatherers. The connection they had to meat was immediate and undeniable – they killed an animal and ate it. Later, they added the process of cooking.

When people began settling in communities and developed farming, their connection to meat was still strong. Many people only ate meat they themselves hunted, while others ate meat that a friend or neighbour had hunted. Meat could be salted, cured, and stored (all forms of processing). Meat could be traded for grains, vegetables, or other needed products. But everyone knew where the meat on the table had come from.

In the 18th and 19th centuries, during a period known as the Industrial Revolution, major changes to agriculture and industry changed how people lived and worked. More people moved into cities and many began working regular – and long – hours in factories. They no longer had time to spend growing and rearing their own food. People began getting more and more removed from their meat.

GUSTAVUS SWIFT

Gustavus Swift (1839–1903) started his meat business with a simple meat market in Massachusetts, USA. He quickly became a cattle buyer, and then a cattle wholesaler (selling cattle to other butchers). Swift is credited with the development of the first useable ice-cooled rail carriage. This car allowed Swift's meat-packing company to ship meat throughout the country, ushering in the era of cheap beef.

Because he owned the cattle, the processing plant, the means of transport, and the market, Swift controlled every aspect of his meat industry. This kind of business plan is known as vertical integration. Today, Swift & Company is the third-largest processor of fresh beef and pork products in the United States and is also the leading beef processor in Australia.

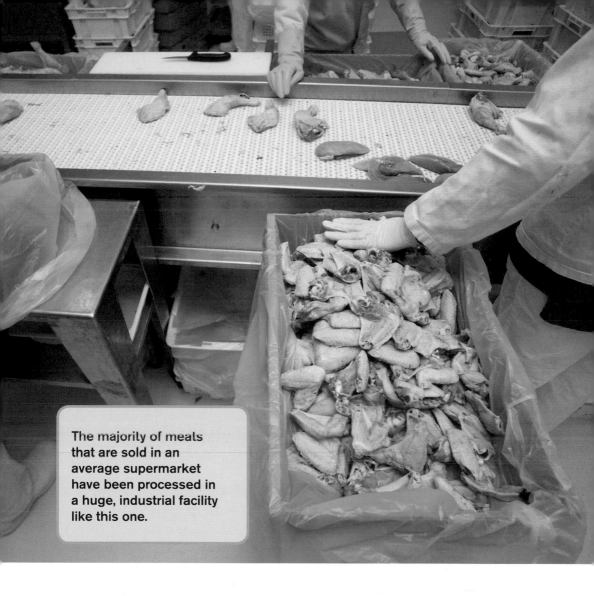

The majority of meals that are sold in an average supermarket have been processed in a huge, industrial facility like this one.

Today, most meat eaters are even further removed from their food. Most people buy meat in large supermarkets, where it has been frozen or pre-packaged into other foods. As we will see, industry and processing have entered every element of the meat we eat, from the way the animals are conceived, to what they are fed, to how they wind up on our plates.

The United States is the world's meat-packing centre, with about 10 billion animals slaughtered there every year. In the European Union, the annual figure is 300 million cattle, sheep, and pigs and 4 billion chickens. Today, just a few processors control most of the market. This gives them the power to control how meat is both reared and processed.

What cows eat

Like all mammals, a baby cow drinks its mother's milk. After being weaned from milk, though, cows are naturally plant eaters. Left to nature, cows will graze in pastures. Cows, sheep, and other animals called ruminants have the ability to turn simple grass, which humans cannot digest, into protein. A cow's rumen (its second stomach) is host to a variety of bacteria that can break the grass down into protein. A cow's manure (waste) provides excellent fertilizer for the grass, so the grass continues to grow—and the whole process continues.

Not cost-effective

As natural as eating and fertilizing grass is, it is not the most cost-effective process for creating meat. This is because grass alone does not allow cows to grow as quickly as if they were fed on other diets. Two generations ago, cows were not slaughtered until they were four or five years old. One generation ago, they were slaughtered at two or three years old. Today, most cows born to become meat have only a 16-month lifespan. This is accomplished by feeding the cow a diet made primarily of corn. Cows do not naturally digest corn, so they also need to be given regular doses of **antibiotics** to aid the digestion process.

When we eat cows that are raised this way, or drink their milk, these antibiotics eventually make their way into our own bodies. Over time, bacteria evolve to resist the antibiotics, so the drugs are no longer effective. Many doctors worry that these new, stronger bacteria could make humans ill. The antibiotics people use to fight illness are often the same ones given to the cows. If the evolved bacteria entered a human, doctors would not have antibiotics strong enough to kill them. Or the drugs that can kill the bacteria are much more expensive than normal antibiotics.

Growth hormones

In the United States, cattle are also fed growth hormones. This causes cows to put on more weight in a shorter period of time. Doctors have expressed concerns that the growth hormones fed to cows are making their way to our bodies, causing issues like increased obesity and early-onset puberty. However, there is no current scientific evidence that hormone-injected cattle will cause human health problems.

The feeding of growth hormones to cattle has been banned in the European Union since 1988. In the UK, the ban was in place in December 1986. The ban also applies to any meat imported into the UK from countries such as the United States.

Health watch

Is corn-fed beef unhealthy?

Even without the antibiotics and hormones, would corn-fed beef still be unhealthy to eat? A growing body of evidence suggests that it would be. The beef from corn-fed cattle has fewer omega-3 fatty acids than grass-fed beef. Omega-3 fatty acids are necessary for human development. They help in brain development and may reduce the risk of heart disease. The human body is not able to make these fatty acids, so they have to be provided by foods.

Another problem with corn-fed beef is that it has more fat than grass-fed beef. Also, because corn-fed cattle often live in small, enclosed pens, they live in their own manure. If their manure contains *E. coli* or other harmful bacteria, it can wind up back on the cow – and thus in the cow's meat. (See page 28 for a tragic example of this danger.)

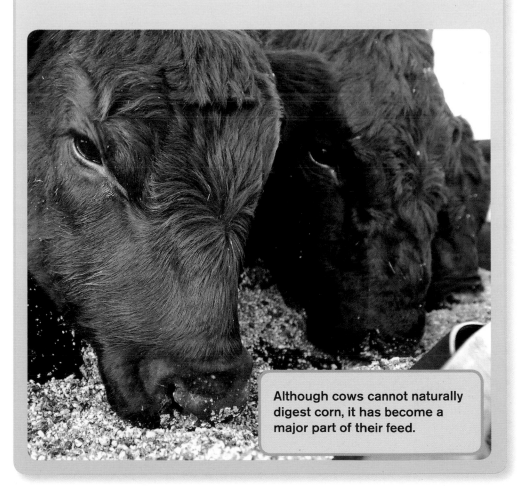

Although cows cannot naturally digest corn, it has become a major part of their feed.

The kill floor

Killing an animal for food will never be pleasant. But modern slaughter practices for animals are so **industrialized** that they have become cruel to animals, unsafe to people who do the work, and unsafe to people who eat the meat.

In an industrial abattoir or slaughterhouse "kill floor", cattle pass onto the floor in a chute that forces them to walk in a single-file line. The walls of the chute are high enough that the animal cannot see much more than the rear end of the cow in front of it. Eventually, they move onto a conveyor belt, much like a moving walkway in an airport. The cows actually straddle this conveyor, rather than standing on it.

In a modern abattoir, the chute that leads to the kill floor is narrow enough that cattle cannot see what lies ahead.

The stunner

Above the belt, on a raised platform, stands a person called a stunner. The stunner carries a pneumatic gun, which uses air power to propel a steel bolt into the head of the animal. Although this person is called a stunner, his or her job is to kill the cow, not just stun it. Unfortunately, the stun does not always kill the cow. There have been reports of cattle waking up farther down the process. A second stunner is available farther down the process to ensure that cattle are killed as painlessly as possible.

After the animal passes the stunner, a worker ties a cord around one of its back legs. The other end of the cord is attached to an overhead trolley, or moving track. The animal is carried upside-down to the bleeding area, where a worker cuts its throat. While reflexes cause the animal to kick and jerk, it is dead at this point.

TEMPLE GRANDIN

Dr Temple Grandin (born 1947) is a professor of animal science who has designed livestock-handling facilities in North America, Europe, and Australia. Grandin's designs draw in part on her own experiences of living with autism. Autism is a disorder that affects the development of the brain. Some people with autism function very well, while others may have extreme difficulty with social interaction and communication. As a child, Grandin often felt overwhelmed by the multitude of sights and sounds surrounding her. She related her own feelings to those of the cattle on the ranch where she was raised. She realized that limiting the sensory experiences the animals were exposed to would help calm them.

Today, Grandin's designs for abattoirs are used to handle half the cattle in the United States. Companies such as Burger King and McDonald's have hired Grandin to observe and assess the slaughter of cattle they own. According to Grandin, since McDonald's became interested in the welfare of its cattle, the process has become more humane.

mo

Temple Grandin at an awards ceremony in 2010. In 2009, a critically acclaimed film, *Temple Grandin*, was released. It told the story of her fascinating life.

Case study:
A terrible tragedy

In the summer of 2001, Barbara and Michael Kowalcyk went on holiday with their four children. Along the way, they stopped for hamburgers and other fast food.

Two weeks after they got home, their two-and-a-half-year-old son, Kevin, started suffering from diarrhoea and a mild fever. When the Kowalcyks saw blood in Kevin's diarrhoea, they rushed him to the emergency room. Doctors discovered Kevin had a form of E. coli, a type of food poisoning named for the bacteria that cause it. *E. coli* is sometimes found in ground meat and other processed foods. While it is dangerous for all people, it is especially deadly to young and elderly people. Twelve days after being admitted to the hospital, Kevin died.

On 1 August, the day after Kevin went to the hospital, the meat packing plant that had processed the beef the Kowalcyks had eaten tested positive for *E. coli* **contamination**. Because of this experience, Barbara Kowalcyk became a food activist, fighting for rules and regulations to improve food safety in the United States.

Kevin's story points out some of the concerns about the safety of processed food. Many people fear that our food processing methods are not always safe. When a problem arises, it is often not detected until after one or more person gets ill. Even then, food **recalls** (removing food products from stores) come too late, or they are ineffective.

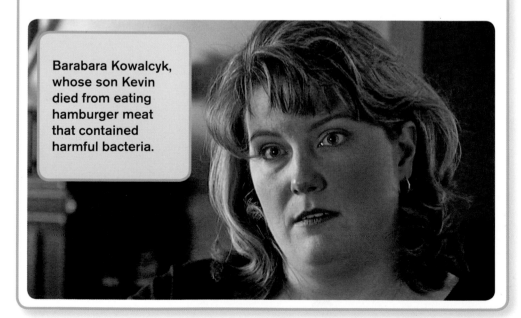

Barabara Kowalcyk, whose son Kevin died from eating hamburger meat that contained harmful bacteria.

Cannibal cows and mad cow disease

The meat products that come from large animals such as cows and pigs represent only part of the process. The rest of an animal's carcass is converted into a host of useful products. This process is called rendering. Until July 1988 much of the product rendered from cattle, including meat and bone meal, was then fed back to the cattle. The theory was that protein was protein, so that even though cows do not naturally eat meat, there was no harm in feeding it to them.

BSE outbreak

In November 1986, two cows from different parts of England were diagnosed with bovine spongiform encephalopathy (BSE). BSE is more commonly known as mad cow disease, because it makes cows act strangely, or as though they were "mad". BSE tends to occur in animals over the age of five and causes symptoms such as strange movements and changes in mental state. If a person eats a cow infected with BSE, he or she can develop a variation of a neurological disease (a disease affecting the brain, nerves, or spinal cord) called Creutzfeldt-Jakob disease.

Epidemic

The epidemic grew rapidly and reached its peak in 1992 when more than 850 new cases were announced every week. At one point 36,680 cases were known in Britain. Since 1992 there has been a steady decline in cases so that there are now fewer than four cases announced each week. Contaminated animal feed was soon discovered to be the cause.

> "Ground beef [mince] is not a completely safe product. Unfortunately it looks like we are going a bit in the opposite direction."
> Dr Jeffrey Bender, a food safety expert quoted in 2009, discussing problems with *E. coli* contamination

However, there are no rules preventing cow products from being made into animal feed for other animals, such as chickens or pigs. Some scientists worry that if a cow with BSE goes undiagnosed, it could infect other animals this way.

The industrialized chicken

The chicken industry is also a marvel of modern food processing. People have been breeding and crossbreeding chickens to develop desirable traits at least since the 1800s. In the late 1800s, the emerging railway network made it easy to transport chickens from hatcheries to market. At the time, most of the chicken industry focused on eggs, rather than chicken as meat.

Health watch

What is a chicken nugget?

Chicken nuggets are a heavily processed food. They were first invented in the 1950s. In 1979 McDonald's commissioned the food-processing company Tyson to create a recipe. The meat is held together with phosphate salts and then fried. Frozen chicken nuggets sold in supermarkets can be made either from white meat or from "mechanically separated chicken (MSC)". MSC is meat that has been mechanically taken off the bones or other parts of chicken. But really, chicken nuggets are more corn than meat. The meat comes from chickens that ate corn, a huge number of ingredients and additives in the nugget itself are corn-based, and even the sauces served with the nuggets are made primarily from corn!

Experts have estimated that average chicken nuggets have around 37 ingredients, and that at least 30 of those ingredients come from corn.

Health watch

Food fight in schools

Many children love chicken nuggets for a quick snack or school time meal. But to some food experts, they're just one of the many processed foods children shouldn't be eating. Many school lunches contain highly processed foods with high levels of fat, sugar, and salt. Some schools have machines that sell similar foods, snacks, and fizzy drinks. Well-known television chef Jamie Oliver has led the battle to improve school lunches both in the UK and in other countries. Oliver made a television series called *Jamie's School Dinners* that resulted in the government setting up the School Food Trust. It meant that more money was spent on nutritious meals in schools. Oliver called for more "naked" foods, meaning fresh fruits and vegetables, and fewer processed foods. He also said students should receive more food education, so they know which foods are the best for them to eat.

In 2010, a group of retired US military officers said that school lunches were making children too fat – and making it harder for the military to find new recruits who met its weight guidelines. Studies by the government strongly suggested that eating school lunches made children fatter. Using fresh ingredients, however, drives up the cost of school meals.

During the two world wars (1914–18 and 1939–45), the government encouraged people to raise chickens at home. A small flock of chickens could be an efficient way to discard table scraps, produce many eggs for protein, and supply meat. A chicken flock is very vulnerable to disease and parasites, so chicken remained much more expensive than other meat until the 1950s. At this point, antibiotics and other drugs began to be used to keep chickens healthy.

Drugs, combined with higher-protein and vitamin-enriched feed, helped create the era of large-scale chicken production that we have today. The chicken industry is estimated to have a total annual value of £1.5 billion. Today, hens are often housed in windowless buildings with many other chickens. Six or seven hens may share a cage so small that they cannot even spread their wings. Hens do not even sit on their own eggs, as incubation (keeping the eggs warm) is done by machine. Like other livestock, chickens are often fed growth hormones to increase their size.

Preservatives in meat

All meat is processed in some way, to get it off the animal and ready to sell. But the term "processed meat" usually refers to meat that is mixed with preservatives of some kind. Some of these meats include hot dogs, lunch meats such as salami and ham, bacon, and a variety of tinned meats.

For example, sausage is one of the oldest forms of processed meats. Sausages are typically made from pork. Traditional sausage is made by putting tissues and organ meat, which is highly fatty and nutritious, into a casing made from the animal's own intestine. Today, the casing is frequently made from other materials such as collagen, cellulose, or even plastic.

Most processed meats have something in common: they have high levels of salt, fat, nitrates, and nitrites. These ingredients preserve the meat and keep it from spoiling, but also add health risks. A recent study suggests that all processed meats increase the risk of heart disease and diabetes, compared to unprocessed red meats such as beef, lamb, and pork. The study showed that the processed meats were four times as salty as the unprocessed meats and contained 50 per cent more nitrates.

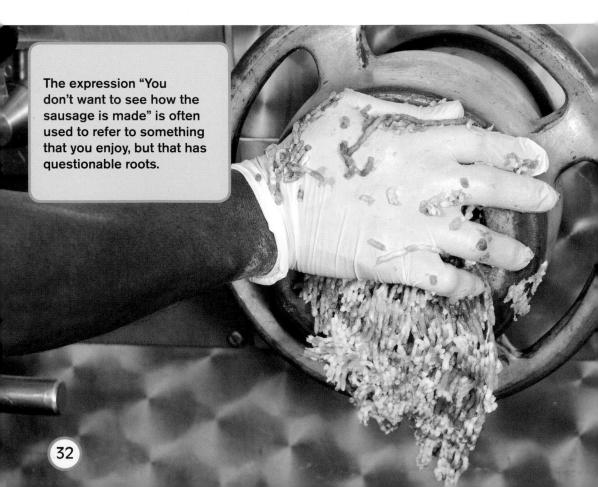

The expression "You don't want to see how the sausage is made" is often used to refer to something that you enjoy, but that has questionable roots.

The nitrates and nitrites in processed meats particularly concern many scientists. In large doses, they can be deadly to humans. Food companies must follow strict rules about how much they put in their meats. But even these so-called safe amounts could lead to health problems. In the body, nitrites combine with certain proteins to create **nitrosamines**. Some of these chemicals cause cancer in animals and could affect humans too. Consuming a lot of nitrates and nitrites has also been linked to other diseases in humans, such as Alzheimer's disease and some forms of diabetes. Some scientists, however, say the fear of getting a serious disease from eating nitrates and nitrites is overstated. Humans eat more nitrates in vegetables than they do in processed meats. Also, one study suggests eating nitrates and nitrites might actually strengthen heart cells.

Health watch

Fake fats

Because animals have fat, animal products are naturally fatty foods. As doctors began to make connections between eating too many fats and health problems such as heart disease, scientists began looking for alternatives to the fats that are naturally present in animal products.

Margarine, a kind of synthetic butter, was first made in 1869. Like many processed foods, it was created to help an army. Margarine was developed for the French army. Armies need to travel with their kitchens, and butter does not keep well without refrigeration. Synthetic or artificial fats are more stable than naturally occurring fats, so they do not require the kind of refrigeration that other fats do. Their structure can be controlled, giving these products a more consistent and reliable texture. They are also cheaper than natural fats.

In the 1990s Proctor & Gamble attempted to create a fat that would not add any calories to foods. The product was marketed as Olestra. Unfortunately, the reason Olestra does not add calories is that it is made of products that humans are not able to digest. Many people became ill after eating foods made with Olestra, but it can still be found in some processed food products.

Dangerous places to work

Abattoirs and the meat-packing industry have been areas of concern for many years, but not just for the treatment of animals. It is one of the most dangerous industries to work in. There are about 90,000 meat-processing workers in the UK. A lot of training is required for all jobs in the industry, but much of it is on-the-job training, which can lead to accidents, particularly if trainees are left unsupervised. Over the years 2005 to 2008, the rate of injury for meat slaughtering per 100,000 workers was 1,054. For poultry slaughtering, the rate was 1,459. The British Meat Processors Association (BMPA) holds meetings about health and safety issues in the industry several times a year.

The human cost

Today, Human Rights Watch has called meat-packing and abattoirs the most dangerous factory jobs in the United States. Part of the problem is that meat-packing is treated as factory work. Workers perform a limited number of tasks, repeating them over and over again. They are often forced to work at a pace that is too fast to be safe. Working conditions are not **sanitary**, and workers often perform their jobs covered in animal blood, urine, and faeces (waste).

Workers can suffer injuries from a slip of the knife, or from repeating the same motion more than 10,000 times a day. They occasionally pass out from the fumes of the chemicals used to process the meat. They have arms or legs crushed by unsafe machinery. They get infections from handling the meat, which results in their fingernails separating from their fingers. Temple Grandin (see page 27) has written that it is not uncommon for full-time abattoir workers to become sadistic, meaning they take pleasure in being cruel. The process of constantly killing other living beings affects a person's behaviour.

Because many of the people who work in these factories are poor, they often do not have other options. Large packing plants tend to suppress workers' efforts to gain rights by forming unions, and they sack workers who support a union. Large meat-packers in the United States regularly advertise for workers in Mexico. If these workers come to the United States illegally, they risk being arrested and deported. The meat-packers and abattoirs that hire illegal workers rarely face significant punishments, even though it is illegal to knowingly hire someone who is not a citizen of the country.

Workers in the meat processing industry have long struggled to gain fair treatment and safe working conditions from their employers. These workers are holding a rally in Chicago, USA, in 1946.

Processing dairy products

Dairy products, another essential part of many people's diets, are the result of many processing steps.

For example, all cheese is processed food made from milk. Farmers used to make cheese at home, but today, cheese is created in a factory. The first step is to pasteurize the milk. Milk is heated to 74 °C (165 °F), killing harmful bacteria. (For more on pasteurization, see pages 38 and 39.) After the milk cools, it is pumped into a stainless steel vat, and a starter culture (or bacteria) is added to the milk. Large robotic arms stir the milk. Rennet, an animal byproduct, is added to the milk to thicken it.

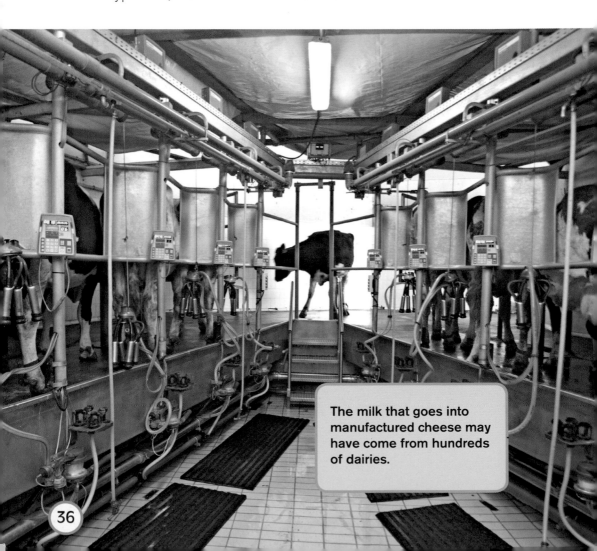

The milk that goes into manufactured cheese may have come from hundreds of dairies.

After curds form, they are mechanically cut into thousands of small cubes. The curds and their whey (a clear liquid) are pumped into a trough-like tub called a finishing table. The curds are mounded into piles and begin to knit into a solid mass.

The whey is drained off and pumped into another machine, where it is condensed, meaning the liquids are removed. The whey is shipped to other processors, where it is used in products like sweets, ice cream, and baked goods. (People with dairy allergies have to read ingredients very carefully, since dairy products like whey may turn up in processed foods that one would not expect to contain milk products.)

The cheese curds are mechanically cut and re-cut and combined with hot water. The cheese is melted into a big, shiny mound and then formed into mounds to cool. The mounds of cheese are soaked in a brine (salty water) bath, which is where different cheeses gain their different flavours. The cheese is then further processed and sold.

Cheese product

While clearly heavily processed and mechanized, the cheese described so far is not that different from cheese made in earlier times. However, what we think of as processed cheese, is a different product altogether.

The now-familiar individually wrapped orange slice of processed cheese was first created in Switzerland by Walter Gerber in 1911. Regulations in the UK mean that the labels have to say "cheese food" or "cheese spread" rather than simply "cheese".

Emulsifiers – substances that bind two different substances together – are added to the cheese product, which makes the cheese melt evenly. Colourings and preservatives are also added so that the cheese lasts longer. For this reason, these types of cheese are popular in cooking and for use with food like cheeseburgers. Processed cheese is not as tasty to eat on its own, however!

Recently, as consumers worry more about the levels of sodium (salt) they eat, research has been carried out to develop a reduced sodium cheese. Scientists at University College Dublin have come up with a processed cheese that has 60 per cent less sodium than normal cheese. Whether the process will become common – and the cheese popular – remains to be seen.

Case study:
Drunk cows and pasteurized milk

Until the mid-1800s in the United States, dairy cows lived on farms or on small patches of land in cities. If people drank milk, it probably came from a cow that lived near them. As cities grew larger, lack of room and sanitation problems meant that fewer cows lived in cities. The first milk brought to New York City by train was in 1842.

Scientist Louis Pasteur made remarkable breakthroughs in discovering the causes of diseases, and in methods of disease prevention.

At that time, most milk was actually coming from cows that lived at alcohol breweries and distilleries. The cows lived there to eat the grain mash that was left over from making beer and alcohol. This feed had very little nutritional value, and as a result the milk from cows that ate it was of very poor quality. The public began to object to the idea of the horrible conditions the cows were kept in, and to the fact that children were drinking milk produced by "drunk cows".

In 1862 New York banned the sale of the "drunk" milk, and many other cities began to follow this example. The solution was to allow cows to live in grassy areas around the city and then transport the milk to the city. But because the source of the milk – farms – was now so far away from the customer, problems began to occur with milk. People created some of these problems. For example, they would add chalk to milk to make it appear whiter and even add poisonous formaldehyde to keep the milk from souring. Milk improperly transported also began to develop and create diseases.

During the late 1800s, German scientist Robert Koch and French scientist Louis Pasteur developed the germ theory of disease. This theory states that tiny organisms such as bacteria, which the scientists called germs, cause many diseases. They discovered that disease could easily be spread by contaminated food. Milk, which arrived from the country daily and was consumed raw, was seen as a cause.

Pasteurizing milk (heating it to very high temperatures to kill the bacteria) was seen as a solution to the problem of diseases spread by milk. In 1909 Chicago became the first city to prohibit selling unpasteurized milk, and other cities followed suit. Later, **homogenization** also became a standard procedure. In this process, the cream (fat) globules in milk are broken up into tiny particles. This keeps a cream layer from forming at the top of milk.

It has been shown that pasteurizing milk not only destroys the germs, but also destroys some of the nutrients. Critics have also worried that because pasteurizing destroys evidence of germs, there is no way to tell if a farm is unsanitary. Other people worry that the very act of pasteurization has added a step, or process, into what used to be a simple food product. Making even the most simple of foods into a product requiring technology alienates us from our food, making it difficult for people to tell the difference between food as it exists naturally and processed food. Because of this, people lose sight of how unhealthy some processed foods can be.

Raw milk and cheese

With products like fluorescent orange "pasteurized prepared cheese product" available in packs in supermarkets, it is no wonder that many people are looking to raw (or "real") milk and raw cheese as more natural alternatives.

Raw milk is the natural, unchanged milk that has not been pasteurized, homogenized, or otherwise heated above the body temperature of the cow. Likewise, raw cheese is cheese that has been made from raw milk. However, while raw milk has to be consumed quickly to prevent spoiling, cheese made from raw milk has to be aged for at least 60 days to allow the acids and salts to kill the bacteria.

Raw milk is not allowed to be sold in shops but can be bought directly from farms, farm shops, and farmers' markets. Some suppliers may also deliver.

Why drink raw milk?

It must be said that some of the interest in raw milk is simply a fad. What people do and do not want to eat goes in and out of fashion in much the same way as clothing.

Health watch

Saturated fat

In 2008, newspaper reports suggested that cigarette-style warnings would appear on food packaging in an attempt to reduce consumption of foods such as cheese and other dairy products. These foods are high in saturated fat, a type of fat that is linked to heart disease, diabetes, and other illnesses. The **Food Standards Agency (FSA)** denied that cigarette-style warnings would be used but admitted that ways of educating consumers about reducing consumption of saturated fat were being researched. A hard-hitting advertising campaign followed in 2009. The FSA stated that people in the UK consume 20 per cent more saturated fat than they should.

However, the dairy industry claimed that they were being unfairly blamed for contributing to rising levels of obesity in the UK. They argued that the benefits of consuming dairy products as part of a healthy lifestyle should be emphasized.

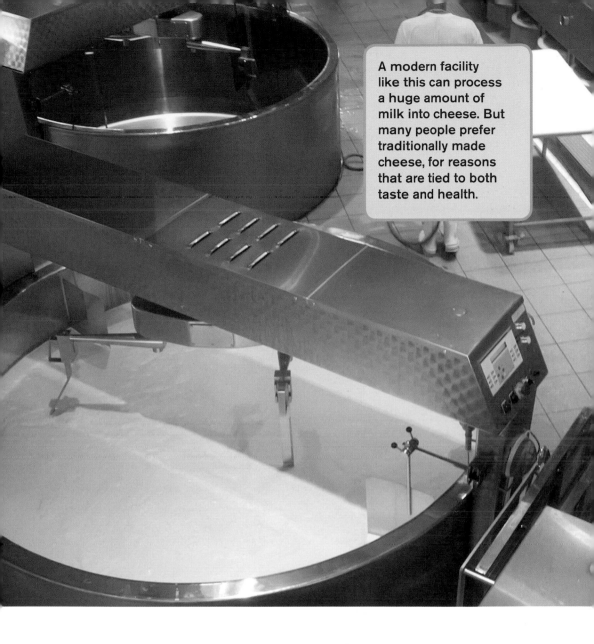

A modern facility like this can process a huge amount of milk into cheese. But many people prefer traditionally made cheese, for reasons that are tied to both taste and health.

But some people are genuinely interested in raw milk as a food that provides excellent nutritional value. Many people are seeking raw milk in an attempt to eat fewer processed foods. Others are concerned about the cows used to make most mass-produced milk. Most milk from dairy farms comes from Holstein cows. These cows have been bred to produce huge amounts of milk – more milk than their own calves need. The way they have been bred has also led to the need to give the cows antibiotics. Many people worry about the dangers posed when humans, especially young people who are still growing, ingest so many antibiotics with their milk.

What does it all cost?

Think about all the products you see at your local supermarket. How many of them are ready-to-eat, processed foods? Just add milk or water, or pop them in the microwave for three minutes, and these foods are ready to go. Better yet, there are shelves and shelves of snack foods people can eat right out of the bag. Some products offer a complete meal, vacuum-sealed and ready to go. Young people on the go or parents looking for a quick meal solution can just drive through their local fast food outlet.

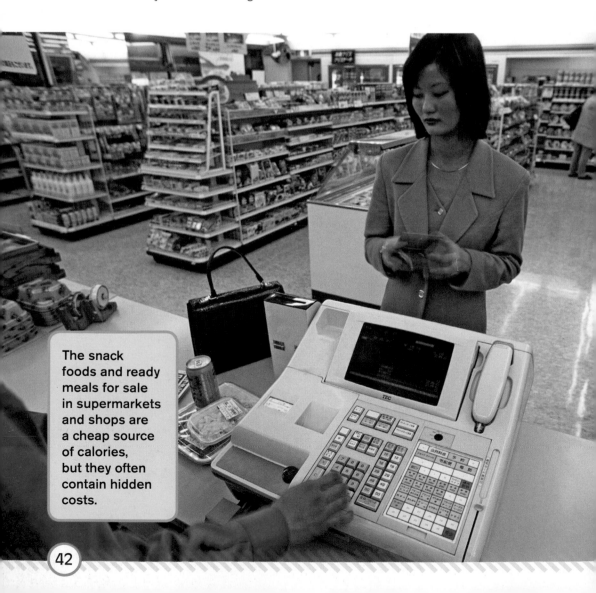

The snack foods and ready meals for sale in supermarkets and shops are a cheap source of calories, but they often contain hidden costs.

These foods are appealing to people with busy schedules, and to families with two working parents and children who are going straight from school to activities. Best of all, this food is cheap. But the foods have a hidden cost, and we are paying the price with our health.

Case study:
Changing the Aboriginal diet

In 1982 nutrition scientist Kerin O'Dea undertook a research project in Western Australia. He recruited a group of 10 Aborigines, the native people of Australia, for his study. These people had all grown up in the Australian bush, and they now lived in and around the town of Derby. All were middle-aged and overweight, and they all suffered some of the health problems commonly associated with a diet of processed food. They were **diabetic**, had high blood pressure, and showed risk factors for heart disease. Their diet was common for the area: processed sugar, processed flour, processed rice, carbonated drinks, meat, and potatoes.

O'Dea accompanied the group back to their native homeland in north-west Australia. There they returned to the eating methods they had grown up with, such as hunting and gathering all of their food. Instead of eating the heavily processed sugars and **carbohydrates** they had grown used to, their diet consisted of fish, birds, and local vegetables.

After seven weeks of this new lifestyle, O'Dea performed a series of tests on his subjects. Their health had improved in every way. All had lost weight. Their blood pressure had dropped. Their **cholesterol** levels had fallen into the normal range. For many of them, their diabetes had completely disappeared. In less than two months, they had regained normal health.

The results were striking. While the increased activity in their new lifestyle no doubt contributed to their improved health, for O'Dea the conclusion was clear. It demonstrated the number of health issues that can be directly linked to diet.

Is processed food cheaper?

One of the reasons processed food is so appealing is because of its cost and convenience. For example, a typical macaroni cheese ready meal that is heated in the microwave or oven costs about £1. It makes a meal in less than 30 minutes.

Environment watch

Packaging

Food packaging is an often-overlooked byproduct of industrial food. It can become damaging to the environment.

Products are often packed in at least two layers of packaging, such as a bag within a box. Individual boxes are packed into larger boxes for shipping, and these boxes are often wrapped in layers of cellophane before being shipped. In the supermarket, fresh items, such as meat, may be packed on a polystyrene tray that is wrapped in plastic. Labelling adds additional paper and glue to the package.

Packaging can even compromise the safety of food. In June 2010, Kellogg's recalled 28 million boxes of children's breakfast cereals after a number of people suffered from nausea and vomiting. The culprit turned out to be the inner liner of the box, which was leaching methylnaphthalene, a petroleum product, into the cereal.

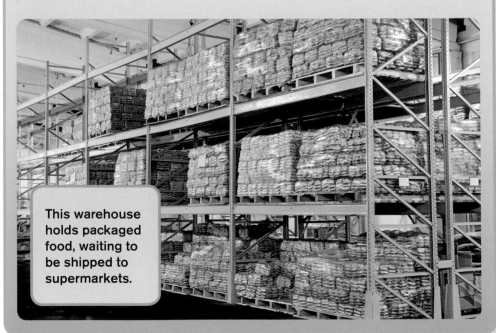

This warehouse holds packaged food, waiting to be shipped to supermarkets.

How does this compare to making macaroni cheese from scratch? Buying the macaroni, cheese, flour, and milk (to make the sauce) separately may seem like it costs more, and it certainly takes more time. But, when divided by serving, it actually is cheaper.

But if people only have £2 to spend, they are better off buying a pre-packaged, processed box. Since they cannot buy the fresh ingredients for the same price, buying the processed foods at least lets them eat dinner. If people are homeless and do not have access to regular refrigeration or storage facilities, they are also better off buying processed food. If people have limited space for food or lack transport to a supermarket, they may also wish to buy smaller pre-packaged foods instead of fresh ingredients.

Health watch

Finding food in a desert

In wealthy areas, shoppers often have a wide range of places where they can buy their food. The largest of them offer tens of thousands of goods, usually at reasonable prices. The story is different, however, in the poor areas of large cities and in some rural areas. These communities are food deserts, meaning residents lack easy access to affordable and nutritious food. In some places, governments offer tax breaks to large supermarkets to place stores in food deserts. But at times, the companies still don't want to come, believing they cannot make enough money in those locations. In many city neighbourhoods, the closest place to buy food is at a tiny corner shop. These shops often lack the room for refrigerators that hold fruits and vegetables, so shoppers can't buy these items fresh. With so little space, the shops only stock items that are popular. For poorer people, that means cheap processed foods. The sugar, salt, and fat in those items make them tasty. But they also make the foods fattening and otherwise unhealthy. To find a better selection of healthy foods at a reasonable cost, shoppers might have to travel many kilometres — a trip that can take several hours if they don't have a car.

Making choices

By now, your head may be spinning. With so many dangers related to processed foods, what is safe? While the concerns are real, the dangers are not always immediate. According to the Food Standards Agency, in 2007 about one million people in the UK suffered a food-borne illness. Of that number, 500 died. By comparison, just under 3,000 people died in car accidents that year.

It is often difficult to know what you are eating in a restaurant. A restaurant may boast that it makes its own sauce, but it may actually use industrial tomato paste filled with preservatives and HFCS as the base of the sauce.

The real dangers, though, are long term. A constant diet of heavily processed sugars and carbohydrates can lead to obesity and other health risks. Especially at high levels in the diet, substances such as high fructose corn syrup (HFCS) can affect the body's ability to regulate sugar levels in the blood. Food dyes and other additives can have negative effects on children — and on all people, to some degree.

Pizza: fresh or processed?

There is nothing about pizza that means it has to be unhealthy. Packed with vitamins and antioxidants, tomato sauce is one of the healthiest things you can eat. A wholewheat crust can provide fibre, and cheese is a valuable source of protein and calcium. Pizza can also be topped with a variety of vegetables, making it a complete meal in one tasty dish.

Unfortunately, pizza can also be turned into a frozen disk filled with unpronounceable ingredients and fat. Frozen pizza is often an example of an unhealthy processed food.

Pizza starts with a crust, and the crust starts with flour. But in a frozen pizza, the wheat in that flour was probably milled, bleached, and enriched long before it made its way anywhere near the pizza.

The frozen pizza is topped with a thick, red tomato sauce. But what exactly is in that sauce, and how does it keep its bright colour? There are probably some tomatoes in there, as well as a large dose of HFCS. There is probably also a lot of salt, citric acid, and calcium chloride, acting as a preservative. Odds are good the colour comes from a food dye.

Let's assume that the frozen pizza is topped with meat — probably sausage, pepperoni, or some other meat product. As we have seen, how an animal is converted into a uniform meat-like substance is a long, and sometimes horrifying, tale. Moreover, this kind of meat is often full of fat and potentially dangerous chemicals.

The final layer of the frozen pizza is cheese. There is a good chance the cheeses used are "cheese products", which means they probably contain many artificial substances — and are also full of fat.

So, all pizzas are not the same. Think about this the next time you crave one. Perhaps you could have fun making your own, fresh pizza at home. This would allow you to control the ingredients used — and to know exactly what you are eating.

What steps can I take?

While avoiding processed food can be a challenge, there are a few simple steps you can take.

Shop the perimeter

A common suggestion for avoiding heavily processed foods in the supermarket is to "shop the perimeter". The outer ring of a supermarket often contains the least-processed foods, such as fruits and vegetables, meat, dairy, and freshly baked bread. The centre aisles tend to contain less-natural creations, such as snacks, cereals, and frozen and ready meals.

Another option is to shop at farmers' markets. Many farms also sell their produce by the roadside or allow you to pick your own. You can also buy fresh meat and fish from local sources, such as a local butcher or fish shop.

Health watch

Vegetarianism and veganism – avoiding processed foods?

For a variety of health, taste, and **ethical** reasons, many people choose to become vegetarians and not eat any kind of animal flesh. Others, called vegans, choose not to eat any animal products at all, such as dairy or eggs. However, even people who follow these diets have not been able to escape processed food.

Fake meats such as veggie burgers and veggie sausages are popular items for people who avoid meat. However, few people bother to read the ingredients. Many "veggie burgers" contain no actual vegetables. Although these products tend to be lower in fat and calories than beef burgers, they may be high in sodium.

It is recommended that people look for "veggie" products with less than 10 grams of protein per serving, as those items tend to contain more vegetables. Higher-protein products are primarily soy and gluten. People with food allergies should read ingredient lists carefully, as many "veggie" products are made from soy, wheat, dairy, and nuts.

What do you think?

Many people choose a vegetarian or vegan lifestyle in an attempt to be healthier. Although the ingredients may be healthier, the food is often no less processed than other packaged foods.

Five ingredients

Read the labels. Some nutritionists say you should eat foods that contain no more than five ingredients. While this may be too difficult, the point is clear. If the package lists more chemicals than recognizable ingredients, it is probably processed beyond recognition!

Get involved

The fact that you are reading this book shows that you want to learn more about processed foods and how they affect you. That is a great start. We can change the way corporations treat our food, but only if we make an effort. The first step is to learn more. The next is to act.

Unsing the internet as a tool, you have access to many resources about food, farming, and product recalls. Many major newspapers have sections devoted to these subjects. Government agencies such as the Food Standards Agency frequently publish information about food safety, nutrition, and food alerts on their websites.

Vote with your wallet

"Processed" does not necessarily mean bad. Many food manufacturers have responded to consumer concerns by changing how they treat the food they process. There are more and more healthy alternatives in products such as snacks and breakfast cereals. The more consumers buy these products, the more likely manufacturers are to keep making them. At the same time, realize that the word "healthy" on the label does not mean that what is inside the package is necessarily good for you.

Processed foods are a fact of our busy lives. It is nearly impossible to learn everything about every piece of food you put into your body, and as a teenager, you may have little control over what foods your parents do and do not buy. But, as with any issue, the more you know, the better choices you can make. This book is a start. The rest is up to you.

Human health and food chains

The information here may be useful in helping you better understand some of the information contained in the book.

In the United States a food pyramid is used to stress fruits and vegetables over meat, dairy, and processed foods. Many people object to the food pyramid because it is highly susceptible to political pressure. People representing the beef industry, for example, pressure those responsible for the pyramid to emphasize the benefits of beef.

The eatwell plate

Use the eatwell plate to help you get the balance right. It shows how much of what you eat should come from each food group.

FOOD STANDARDS AGENCY
food.gov.uk

The "eatwell plate" shows how much of different types of food a person should consume in order to have a healthy, balanced diet .

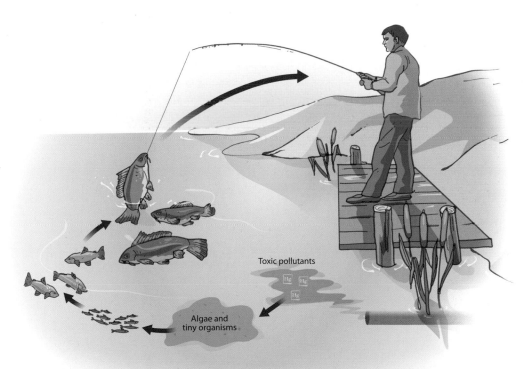

Because humans eat other animals, they are at the top of the food chain. This in turn means that anything that happens to items lower in the food chain also happens to people. For example, some fish swim in waters that have high levels of mercury, a poisonous metal. The mercury enters their bodies and humans can eat it if the fish are caught for food.

Timeline

Approximately 8000 BCE	Beer and bread are the first processed foods
Early 16th century	Corn (maize) is grown for the first time in Europe (see earlier note about the date on page 12)
1809	Canning process is developed in France to preserve food
1869	Artificial butter, called margarine, is invented
1878	Gustavus Swift begins development of first refrigerated train carriage to preserve fresh meat
Late 1800s	Robert Koch and Louis Pasteur develop the germ theory of disease
1950s	Chicken nuggets invented
1961	The Chorleywood Bread Process is developed in the UK. It allows a reduction in the time taken to make a loaf and more homegrown wheat to be used. By 1970, 75 per cent of loafs are made using the process.
1985	Ban on the sale of raw milk in UK shops and supermarkets. It can still be bought directly from farmers.
1986	The feeding of growth hormones to cattle is banned in the UK. Ban applies to imported cattle too.
1999	Scientists develop the first strain of golden rice, which contains added vitamin A
2003	Report released stating people consume too much salt in their diet. It recommends a reduction in salt consumption to 6g a day for adults.

Glossary

additive chemical or other substance added to a food during processing, often used to help preserve the food

antioxidant element that slows or prevents oxidation, a process that transfers electrons from a substance. Oxidation can cause "free radicals", which may cause disease.

bran outer coating of a cereal grain

carbohydrate one of three major nutrients the human body needs to survive, found in fruits, vegetables, beans, and grains

cholesterol waxy substance produced by the body and also found in some foods; high levels in the body can cause heart disease

contamination state of having a harmful or bad substance present

cure treat a food with a chemical or a process that helps preserve it

developed country nation with high average income and large industries

developing country nation in the process of building industries and raising the income level of its citizens

diabetic having the disease diabetes, which results when the body produces too much of, or doesn't properly use, the chemical insulin

E. coli bacteria found in the digestive tract that can cause disease

enrich in food, to add nutrients that were lost during processing

ethical relating to principles of what is right or wrong

fatty acid substance found in some fats that can affect the health of humans

fermentation conversion of sugar to carbon dioxide and alcohol by adding yeast

fibre substance found in grains, fruits, and other foods that aids digestion and has health benefits

Food Standards Agency (FSA) organization responsible for food safety and food hygiene across the UK

fortified strengthened. In food, fortified foods have had vitamins and minerals added to them.

fructose naturally occurring, simple sugar found in honey and many fruits

genetically modified (GM) organism that has had its genes altered to promote certain qualities

germ central part of a grain, found inside the kernel

high fructose corn syrup (HFCS) type of sugar made from corn using an industrial process

homogenization mechanical process that breaks up the cream (fat) globules in milk into very tiny particles, to keep a cream layer from forming

hormone chemical either produced in a living organism or added to it through food or injection, which affects cells

industrialized featuring the widespread use of machines and technology to produce a variety of goods

kernel inner part of a grain used to make flour

mill to take a raw grain and turn it into flour

neurological relating to an organism's system of nerves

nitrosamines harmful chemicals created in the body when nitrites combine with certain proteins

obesity body weight that is much greater than what is healthy or average

organic farming method that does not use chemicals to fertilize crops; also refers to crops produced this way

partially hydrogenated oil oil used in cooking that has been altered so it is solid or partially solid, instead of liquid

pasteurize process of heating milk or other food products to kill bacteria

preservative chemical that helps keep a food from spoiling

protein one of the major chemical nutrients humans need to live

recall removing food products from shops because of a health concern

sanitary clean enough to promote good health

sodium scientific name for salt, which comes in many forms

synthetic made by humans through some sort of chemical process

trans fat type of unhealthy fat found in partially hydrogenated oils

Further information

Books

Eyewitness: Food (Dorling Kindersley, 2006)

Food and Farming: From Food to Table, Richard and Louise Spilsbury (Wayland, 2009)

Food: Ethical Debates in What We Eat, Jim Kerr (Evans Brothers, 2008)

Global Questions: Is Our Food Safe?, Carol Ballard (Franklin Watts, 2008)

Making Healthy Food Choices: Do You Know What's in Your Food?, Neil Morris (Heinemann Library, 2006)

Making Healthy Food Choices: Do You Know Where Your Food Comes From?, Neil Morris (Heinemann Library, 2006)

Sustainable World: Food and Farming, Rob Bowden (Wayland, 2007)

Trends in Food Technology (series), Hazel King; Anne Barnett (Heinemann Library, 2008)

What Do You Think? Is Organic Food Better?, Andrew Langley (Heinemann Library, 2009)

What If We Do Nothing?: Food Safety, Carol Ballard (Franklin Watts, 2009)

Websites

www.nhs.uk/Livewell/healthy-eating/Pages/Healthyeating.aspx
The National Health Service (NHS) site provides resources for better understanding how to choose the best foods to eat.

www.nutrition.org.uk
The British Nutrition Foundation provides lots of information about healthy eating and nutrition, including a section on food in schools.

www.food.gov.uk
The Food Standards Agency is an independent government department that looks into public health and food-related issues.

www.grainchain.com/14-to-16/Default.aspx
Learn about how bread is produced.

Index